THE
ELEVATOR
ESCALATOR
BOOK

A TRANSPORTATION FACT BOOK

BY BOB BARNER

DOUBLEDAY
New York London Toronto Sydney Auckland

FOR MARY AND LIZA

Published by Doubleday,
a division of Bantam Doubleday Dell Publishing Group, Inc.
666 Fifth Avenue, New York, New York 10103

Doubleday
and the portrayal of an anchor with a dolphin
are trademarks of Doubleday,
a division of Bantam Doubleday Dell Publishing Group, Inc.

Library of Congress Cataloging-in-Publication Data

Barner, Bob.
   The elevator/escalator book.
   Summary: The ways twelve different forms of transportation work are explained as a large, brown dog takes each
on a trip to deliver a package.
   1. Transportation—Juvenile literature.   [1. Trans-
portation] I. Title.
TL147.B28 1990   629.04   89-26033

ISBN 0-385-26666-9
ISBN 0-385-26667-7 (lib. bdg.)
R.L. 3.3

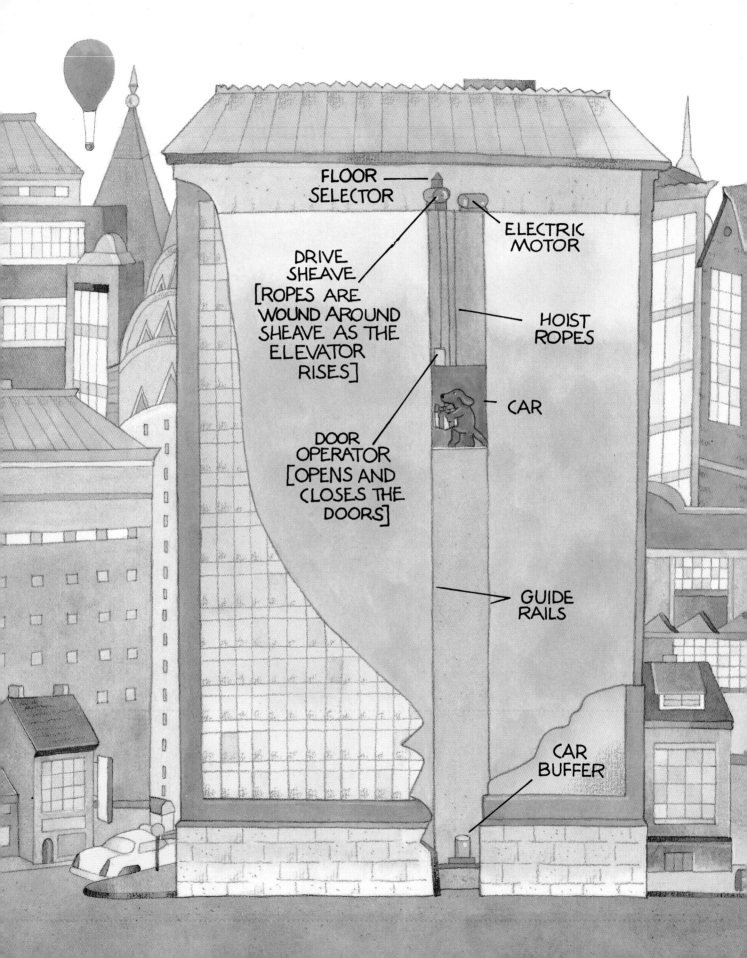

FLOOR SELECTOR

ELECTRIC MOTOR

DRIVE SHEAVE [ROPES ARE WOUND AROUND SHEAVE AS THE ELEVATOR RISES]

HOIST ROPES

CAR

DOOR OPERATOR [OPENS AND CLOSES THE DOORS]

GUIDE RAILS

CAR BUFFER

An elevator is a box that moves up and down a vertical shaft. Most elevators are powered by an electric motor. When the passenger presses a button, the elevator doors close, and the box, which is also called a car, moves up or down to take its passenger to his floor.

A thick rope made of hundreds of small wires, called a cable, is attached to the car. The cable is pulled up or slowly released by the motor. When the elevator reaches the proper floor, the car stops and the doors open. Elevators in some skyscrapers can travel over 500 feet per minute.

A taxicab is similar to a family car. It weighs about 3,000 pounds and has over 14,000 parts. Taxis are popular in large cities all over the world. A taxi driver can take you directly from one place to another, door to door service. Passengers are charged for their ride by the distance traveled and time spent in the taxi. The longer the ride, the more money the driver is paid. The driver must have a special license to drive the taxi.

Passengers usually give the driver a tip for good service.

An escalator is a moving stairway with folding steps. The stairway is an endless loop of steps pulled by chains driven by sprockets that are powered by an electric motor. Sprockets are big wheels with teeth that fit into the spaces in the chains. When the steps reach the new level, the passengers get off and the steps fold flat and return to the lower level to start the trip again.

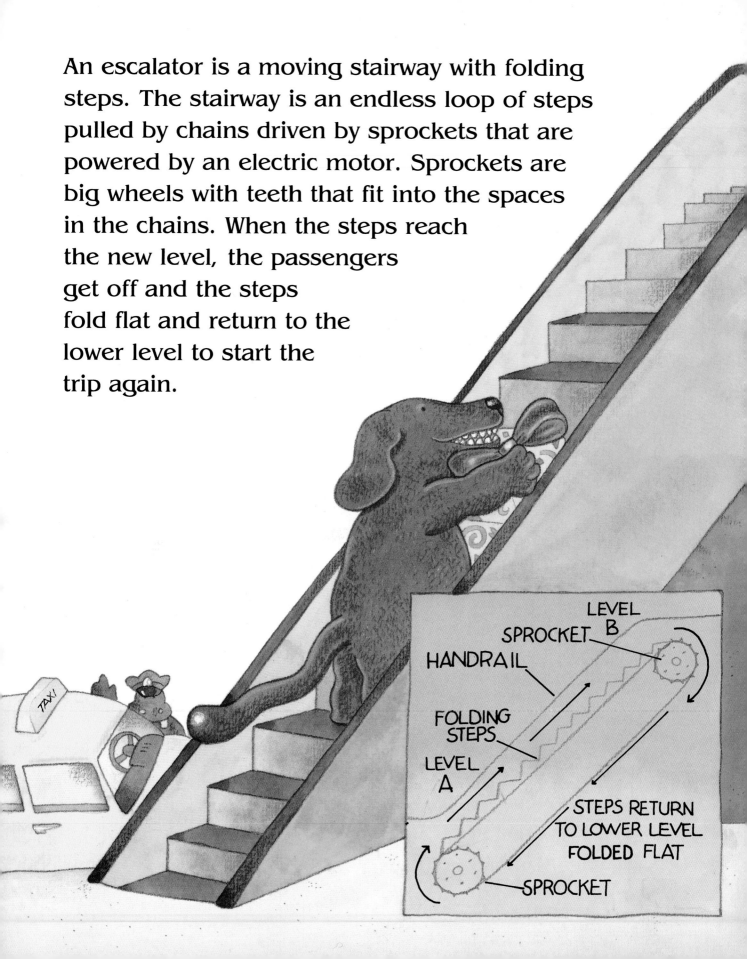

LEVEL B

SPROCKET

HANDRAIL

FOLDING STEPS

LEVEL A

STEPS RETURN TO LOWER LEVEL FOLDED FLAT

SPROCKET

TAXI

Airports and jetports are usually located near big cities. Airports are used for airplane and helicopter takeoffs and landings. The largest airports are several square miles in size and have runways over two miles long. Before boarding the airplane, passengers have their baggage loaded on the plane. Modern airports have restaurants, newsstands, and gift shops. O'Hare International Airport in Chicago is the busiest in the world with over 800,000 takeoffs and landings each year.

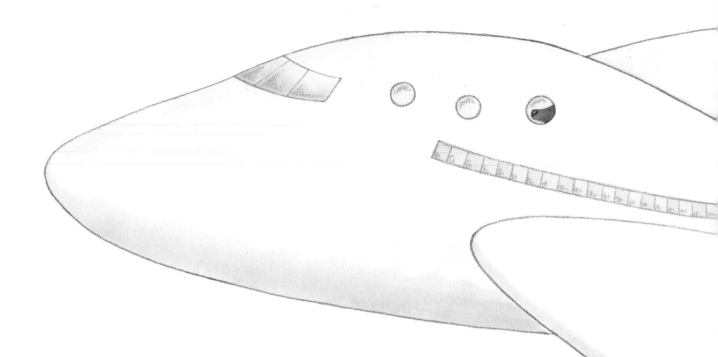

Most passenger airplanes have powerful jet engines that run on special jet fuel. Airplanes with jet engines usually fly over 600 miles per hour and up to 8 miles high. They often fly above thunderstorms to avoid bumpy air.

The pilot and co-pilot fly the plane. They talk to airports by radio and receive weather and air traffic reports.

Flight attendants serve food and make the passengers comfortable during the flight. Airplanes can fly the 3,000 miles from New York City to Los Angeles, California, in about five and a half hours. Airplanes are one of the most popular ways to travel. Over one million people fly in airplanes in the United States each month.

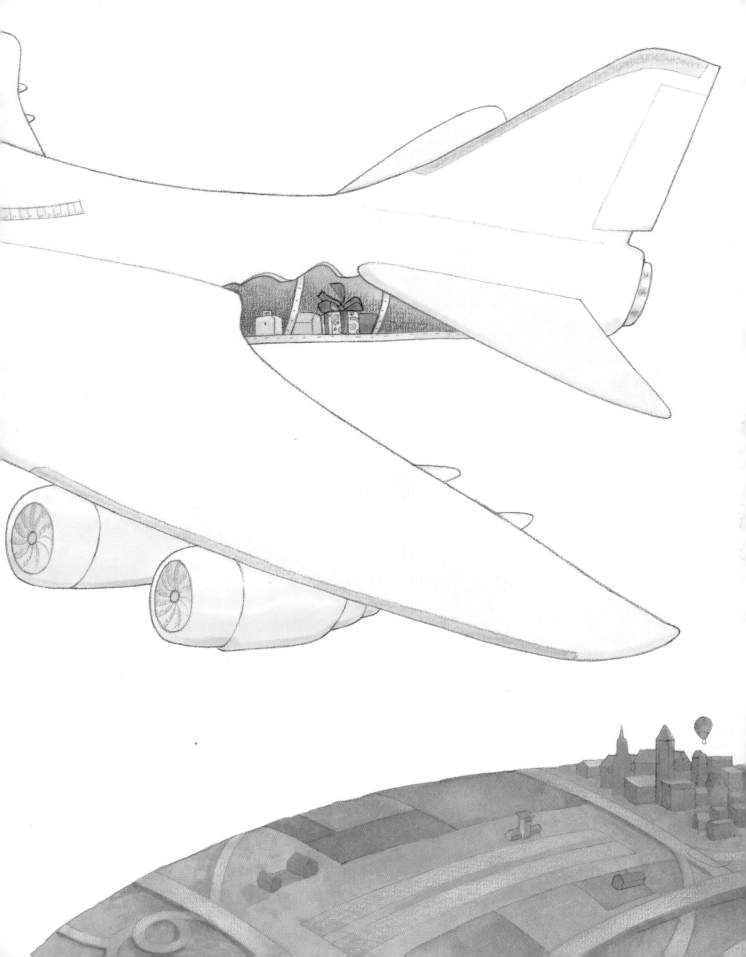

Lights help the pilot see the runway at night and in bad weather.

BAGGAGE

A moving sidewalk is like a giant conveyor belt. The sidewalk is made of thick rubber and is moved by big rollers. Moving sidewalks are used in airports, shopping malls, and other buildings with very large spaces. The first moving sidewalk in America was built at the Columbian Exposition in Chicago in 1893.

Passengers wait for
the bus at a bus stop.
The buses are marked
with signs which tell
where they are going.

An average bus weighs about 25,000 pounds, seats about 60 people and is about 50 feet long. There are over 400,000 buses in the United States. School buses, city buses and buses used for long trips are the most common. Buses travel a route and keep a schedule. Buses used for long trips have air conditioning and bathrooms.

Aerial tramways are used in many of the mountainous areas of Europe and the United States. Passengers ride in a metal car that hangs by grooved wheels from a support cable. The car is moved along by a moving cable that is pulled by an electric motor.

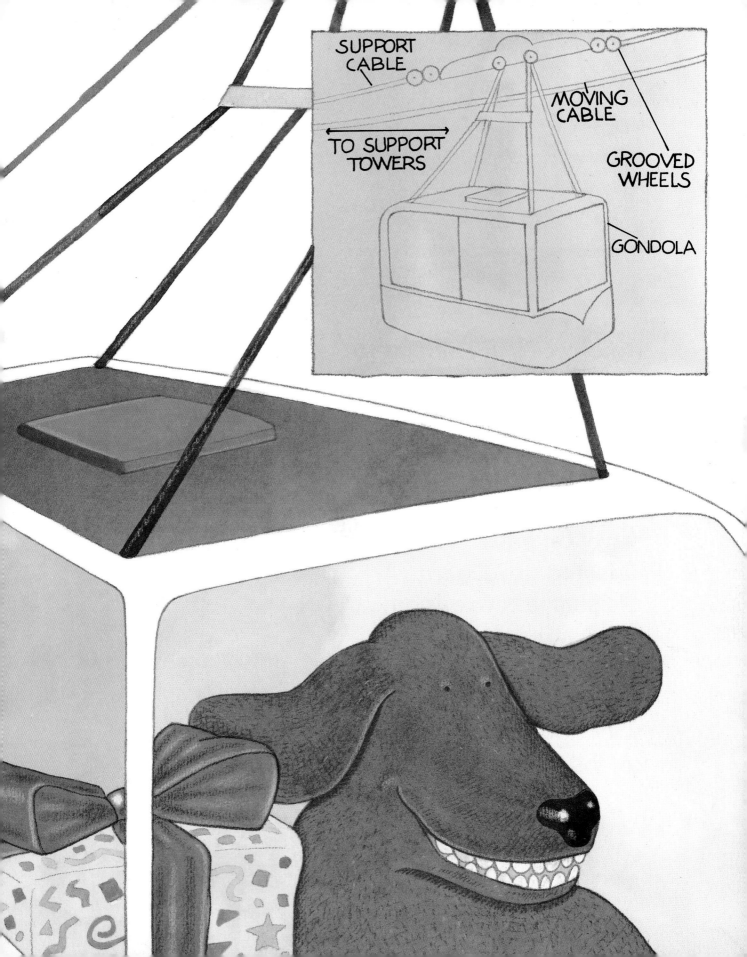

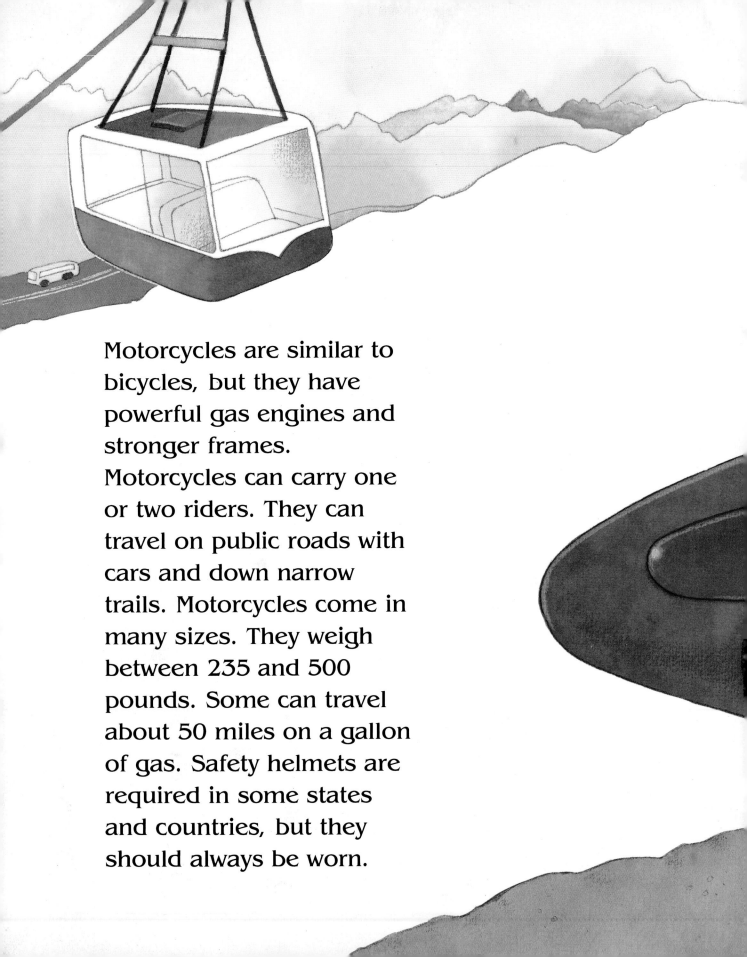

Motorcycles are similar to bicycles, but they have powerful gas engines and stronger frames. Motorcycles can carry one or two riders. They can travel on public roads with cars and down narrow trails. Motorcycles come in many sizes. They weigh between 235 and 500 pounds. Some can travel about 50 miles on a gallon of gas. Safety helmets are required in some states and countries, but they should always be worn.

People who ride motorcycles are called cyclists.
The driver can bring along a friend in a sidecar.

Subways are underground trains. They are
built underground to avoid city crowds and
traffic. Passengers walk down stairs or take
escalators down to the subway tunnels.
Some subway tunnels are 80 feet below the

surface. The trains have electric engines and ride on train tracks. New York City has the world's largest system with over 200 miles of track. The first subway in the United States was built in Boston, Massachusetts, in 1897.

Subways deliver passengers to airports, bus stations, ship docks, and train stations, so they can continue their trips.

A ferry is a boat that carries passengers and cargo across a river, lake, or other body of water. Ferries travel a set route and keep a schedule just as a plane or bus. Cars, trucks, and trains are often carried on ferries.

Some of the largest ferries can carry up to 3,000 people.

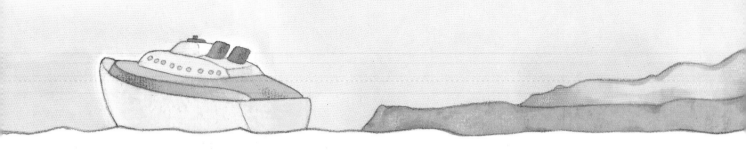

Bicycles have two wheels and a hollow metal frame. The rider moves the bike by pushing the two pedals with his feet. The pedals turn a sprocket which moves a chain. The chain turns the rear wheel which moves the bike forward. The rider steers with the handlebars. Many of the first bikes had no pedals, and were too heavy and hard to ride. In 1840, pedals were attached to a bike called a Dandy Horse. This was the first bike made like modern bikes.

Bicycles are used for racing, making deliveries, fun and exercise. In Southeast Asia, China, and Holland, bicycles are the most popular form of transportation.

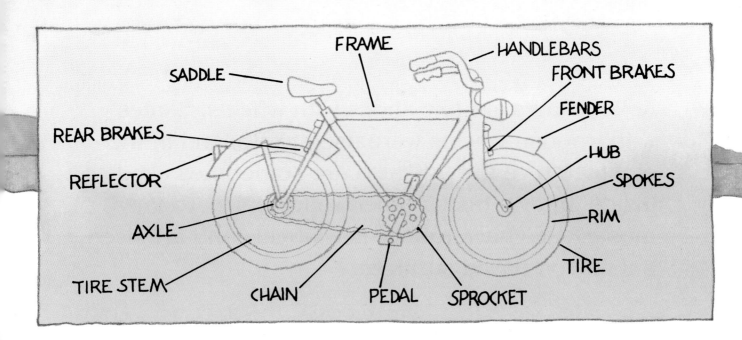

SADDLE — FRAME — HANDLEBARS — FRONT BRAKES — FENDER — HUB — SPOKES — RIM — TIRE — SPROCKET — PEDAL — CHAIN — TIRE STEM — AXLE — REFLECTOR — REAR BRAKES

A bicycle that has two seats is called a tandem bicycle.

Roller skates are like shoes with wheels. Skates with wooden wheels were used in Holland in the eighteenth century. Skates are sometimes used inside on oval tracks called roller rinks. Today most skates have rubber-like wheels and are used outside on paved surfaces.

THE END

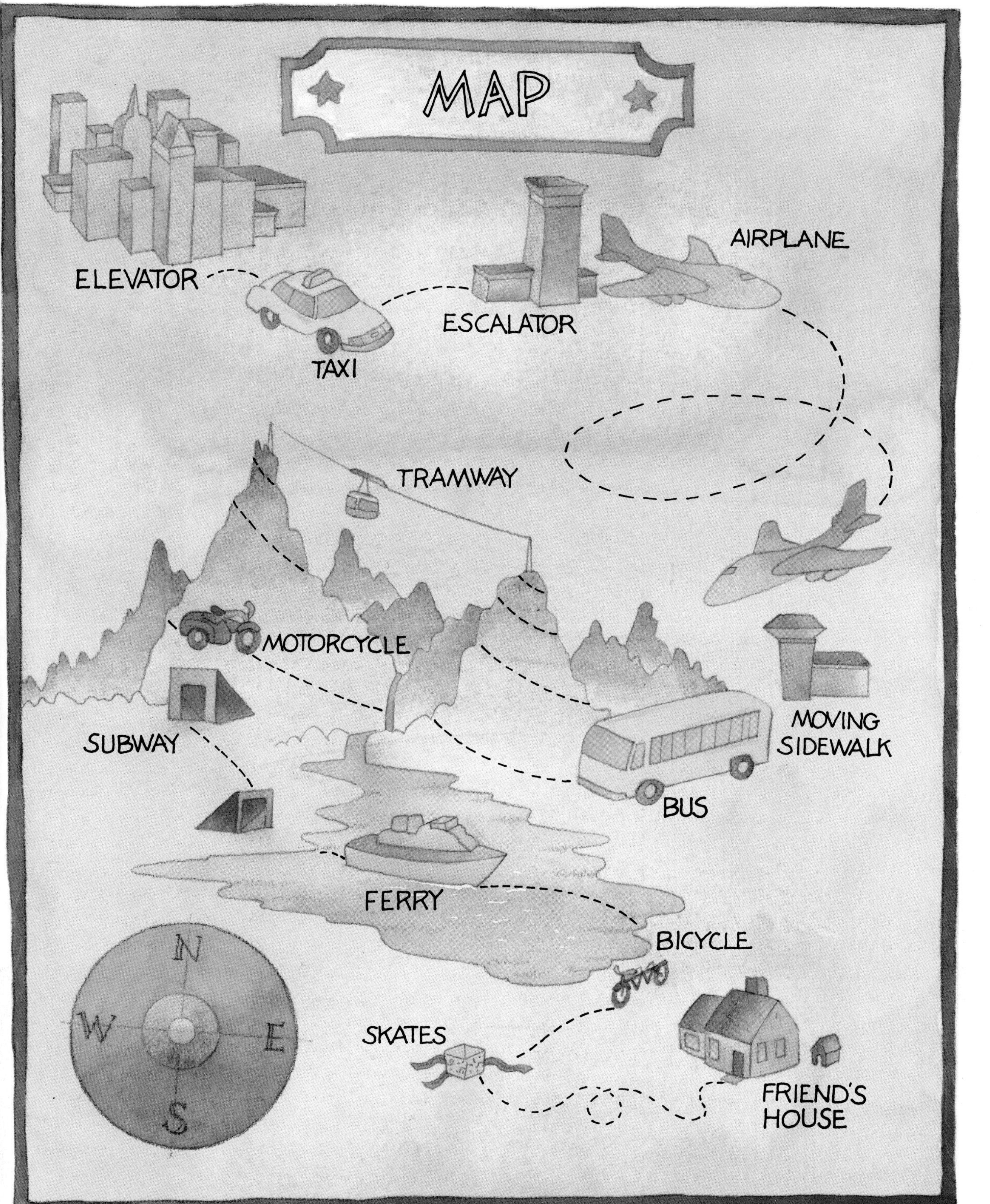

MAP

ELEVATOR

TAXI

ESCALATOR

AIRPLANE

TRAMWAY

MOTORCYCLE

SUBWAY

BUS

MOVING
SIDEWALK

FERRY

BICYCLE

SKATES

FRIEND'S
HOUSE

N
W   E
S

Travel Notes

With all the many kinds of transportation available today, you can travel almost anywhere. You can take short trips that might last only a few minutes, such as riding your bike to a friend's house or taking a bus to school. You might also take longer trips across your state, across the whole country, or even around the world. However, any trip no matter how short must be planned. Long trips can take a lot of planning. Some important things to do before you go on a long trip are buying tickets, studying maps, finding out what kind of weather you're likely to have on your trip, making lists of things you'll need to take, and packing. To travel to another country you may need official papers such as a passport or a visa. Although they are not as complicated as long trips, you should also plan short trips. Make sure you know how to get to your destination and back again. Be sure to take everything you need, including things like bus fare to get home or a coin to call someone to pick you up. You should always travel with an adult unless you are told it's okay to travel alone.